HOW TO FIND YOUR PASSION
DISCOVER AND APPLY YOUR LIFELONG DREAMS

By DAVID A. HUNTER

Text Copyright © 2013 DAVID A. HUNTER

All Rights Reserved

No part of this book may be reproduced
in any way without the written
permission of the author.

Cover Design By David A. Hunter

Disclaimer:
The views expressed within this book are those of the author alone. The information contained within this book is based on the opinions, observations, and experiences of the author and is provided "AS-IS".

No warranties of any kind are made. Neither the author nor publisher are engaged in rendering professional services of any kind. Neither the author nor publisher will assume responsibility or liability for any loss or damage related directly or indirectly to the information contained within this book.

The author has attempted to be as accurate as possible with the information contained within this book. Neither the author nor publisher will assume responsibility or liability for any errors, omissions, inconsistencies, or inaccuracies.

Table of Contents

Is it Necessary to Achieve Your Lifelong Dreams?
How to Achieve Fulfillment By Putting Passion Into Your Daily Life
How to Uncover The Passions That Are Hiding Within You
How to Decide Which Passions You Should Give Priority To
The Importance of Trying New Things and Giving Them a Chance
The Number One Thing You Need to Do to Turn Your Desires into a Career
How to Prevent Your Passion from Fading Away
Understanding The Reason for Your Lifelong Dreams
More from David A. Hunter

Is It Necessary To Achieve Your Lifelong Dreams?

Everything about passion is intense. It involves love, fear, confusion, restlessness, frustration, happiness, and fulfillment.

Passion can seem complex because it comes along with so many positive and negative emotions. Actively pursuing your passion can feel overwhelming at first, but the good news is that many of the negative emotions can be overcome once you learn how to handle them.

I believe that every individual was placed on this earth for a specific reason. I also believe that each person is responsible for fulfilling their purpose in life.

The trouble is that our purpose in life is not always clear to us. To complicate things even more, there is usually an intense fear that comes along with pursuing our passions in life after we have discovered what they are.

Not being able to recognize our lifelong dreams is like not being able to recognize that we are alive.

We can keep forcing ourselves to go in the opposite direction of where we need to be, but it will leave us unfulfilled and without purpose. We can keep ignoring our call to action, but we will miss out on the greatest experiences of our lives. We can keep allowing fear to get in the way, but we will never be able to know what true happiness is.

Finding your passion can bring you excitement, while living your passion will provide you with a huge sense of adventure and accomplishment.

You can still add value to the world without being extremely passionate about what you're doing, but you will be selling yourself short. Even though you are servicing others, you will be doing a disservice to yourself.

A life without passion can seem bland and fake.

You will always feel claustrophobic inside a shell that you don't belong in. Turtles have their own unique advantages, but if you are an eagle, you are meant to fly!

The water might feel intimidating to a dolphin, but he won't survive on the land. You might not literally die if you don't take the right direction, but you certainly won't feel very alive.

Warning signs pop up when we go in the wrong direction, but we usually ignore them. We are told to keep traveling down the dead-end road with everyone else and to not even think about exploring.

We are not encouraged to pursue our different passions when we are growing up. We are forced to read textbooks that we don't want to read, complete assignments that we are uninterested in, and take tests that do not help us.

The things that work for others might not work out the same way for you at all.

Mindlessly following what everyone else is doing will get you lost. You need to take deliberate action in your life if you wish to achieve your lifelong dreams.

There is a plan that has been specifically designed for you. We are not meant to be just another cog in the wheel.

We are destined for amazing things.

Personally, I found several of my main passions when I was 14 years old and I have never looked back. I didn't know for sure what was going to happen, but I knew that I was on the right track, and that's all that really mattered. As long as you're on the right path, persistence will eventually pay you back.

Passion gives you unlimited potential to reach your goals. Passion gives you the motivation to keep trying, even if you fail time after time.

Dreams and desires are within us for a reason. It makes no sense to hold them back by convincing ourselves that "It just can't happen."

You might be able to escape fear by not pursuing your purpose in life, but the fear will soon be replaced by depression and regrets.

<u>Here is what achieving your lifelong dreams can do for you:</u>

- Fulfills your purpose in life
- Gives your life much deeper meaning
- Gives you more energy to face the day
- Brings you joy and satisfaction
- Gives you assurance that you are doing the right thing
- Makes it easier to get up in the morning
- Allows you to help countless people
- Gives you hope for the future
- Gives you incredible confidence
- Gives you a feeling of success even if you fail initially

Unfortunately, it doesn't automatically eliminate fear.

It's not uncommon to second-guess yourself while you are pursuing your passion.

Fear can creep up on you even when you are heading in the right direction, but don't let it discourage you.

I'm sure that you can think of at least one time when you were worried about something only to realize that you were worrying for nothing.

Don't get me wrong. There will always be obstacles on your path, but that's no reason to not walk down the path altogether.

Once you find your passion, you need to stick with it and never give up. With or without fear, you will always be more productive doing work that fulfills you.

There will usually be obstacles on every path, so it makes sense to stick to the one that will make you the happiest.

But it's more than just achieving personal happiness. It's more than just doing what's right for you. Pursuing your passion is also about doing what's right for others.

Having a passion for something is like a gift, but you don't have to keep that gift all to yourself.

To illustrate, a personal fitness trainer will not be able to help someone to the best of their ability if they don't even have a passion for fitness. Showing up to work on time and getting the job done is one thing, but truly making a difference in the world is another thing. You can still work hard and make money, but there will always be a nagging, persistent feeling that something crucial is simply missing from your life.

You can force yourself to do a pretty good job doing things that you don't really like, but think of how much more helpful you can be when you are actually passionate about the work that you are doing.

How To Achieve Fulfillment By Putting Passion Into Your Daily Life

Passion is not just about the type of work that we do. It's much better to fill your entire life with passion.

Before you get completely involved in a career that you are passionate about, it's important to practice having a passion for your life in general. If you are only passionate about work, you might risk turning yourself into a workaholic.

The more things you are passionate about in your life, the more it will spread into other areas of your life. It becomes contagious in a good way.

The number one thing you have to do to invite passion into your life is to embrace your surroundings. Embrace the situations that you go through. Embrace your environment. Embrace the music that you listen to.

Don't waste time by watching a mediocre movie that you know you don't really care for.

Try to pick out the best movie that you can, and when you watch it, get into it. If you can't get yourself into the movie, it's probably not worth watching. It's usually easier to get into a serious movie with a lot of drama than it is to get into a comedy movie.

That doesn't mean you have to completely eliminate comedy movies though. Simply focus on watching more movies that have a deep meaning and make the rest of the movies a second choice, not a priority.

If you are unable to embrace the things in your life that you surround yourself with, it's time to find new surroundings. There might be some things in your life that you are stuck with for right now, but that doesn't mean that you can't start looking for other things. Make the best of the things that you can control.

Here are some examples of what you can do to get started:

- Take pride in your appearance
- Listen to your favorite music daily
- Get fresh air and take walks
- Set aside some time each night to think deep or meditate
- Expect big things to happen

Allow your imagination to lead you to excitement. There are plenty of possibilities out there and small things can turn into big things. It is always possible to breathe life into something dull and bland.

A pen might seem dull at first, but when you're a writer, it becomes a powerful sword. When you look at a stove, don't just see it as a part of the oven. Think about the fire. Now think about the power that the fire has. Fire has the power to help you or burn you. So when you see a stove, see power.

- Be creative
- Use your imagination

- Practice gratitude

How To Uncover The Passions That Are Hiding Within You

Most people have more than one thing that they are passionate about. You don't have to settle for one individual thing. You might not be able to give everything your undivided attention all at the same time, but you can always look for a way to make everything fit.

For example, if you are passionate about music, but you would also love to be a firefighter, you can keep your job as a firefighter and use your days off to work on your music.

As long as you are passionate about both of these things, you will be much less likely to feel overworked.

That's the good thing about pursuing your passion. It doesn't have to feel like a job. Even though you will still experience stress from time to time, you will know that it's worth it. You will have a feeling that everything will work out soon enough.

The worst type of stress usually comes from being overworked at a job that you don't want to have. It becomes a double mistake. Not only are you stressed out, but you're in the wrong career as well. It feels twice as bad.

Pursuing your passion can involve a lot of stress, but there is a good feeling that comes along with being in the right place. It also gives you more patience to deal with problems when they arise.

If you really want to uncover your passion, you will need to change your perspective. If you have been struggling to discover your purpose in life, it is probably because you have been looking at things the wrong way.

Even if you are not looking at things the wrong way, simply looking at things a different way can bring new possibilities to your attention.

The first thing you will need to do is clear your mind and block out any distractions. Try to go to a quiet place that will allow you to think.

Be creative and find a place that really appeals to you. I used to love going to the park in the fall. After summer had ended, there would be almost no one there. This would allow me to really think deep and focus.

You can also go to a library. Just don't do anything dangerous. Don't go out into the middle of the woods by yourself or anything like that.

Taking a vacation would be even better, but it's not necessary. Whatever you decide to do, be patient. If something doesn't click the first time, just try again the next day.

Take the time to think about the things that you would like to do. The trick is to eliminate all of the potential obstacles in your mind for now. You can sort out the problems later, but for now, just focus on the things that you would really like to do without holding yourself back in any way.

For example, if you want to be a rock star, don't automatically dismiss the idea just because you believe that it won't happen. Ignore the obstacles that pop up and just keep thinking about all of the things that you would really like to do.

These questions can help you through the process:

- If I looked back at my life, what would I be the most proud of?
- What makes time pass by really fast for me?
- Who are some of my favorite heroes, and why do I admire them?
- What makes me feel miserable, and how can I avoid that?
- If I had more than enough money, which interests would I be free to pursue?
- What do I want more than anything?

How To Decide Which Passions You Should Give Priority To

The next step is to decide which passions are the most important to you. This is the step where you need to take a serious look at your future. It's time to take a closer look at what you really want out of life.

There might be certain things that excite you in the present time, but you need to think about how you might feel a couple of decades from now.

Working on cars can be fun when you are 20 years old, but would you still be willing to hunch over a car 20 years from now after you have developed back problems from hunching over cars for so long?

I don't want to discourage you, but this is the step where you need to get realistic. If you want to make a good decision as far as choosing the right passions to focus on, you need to practice self-awareness.

Recognizing your strengths is important, but you must recognize your weaknesses as well. Nothing is an overnight process.

Give yourself as much time as you need. Spend some time each day putting your life on pause and just watch and observe. Find out what's really preventing you from moving forward.

Once you understand who you are, things will become much more clear. Try to describe yourself in an honest way, but don't use more than one word at a time.

Here are some examples:

- Leader
- Follower
- Artist
- Provider
- Helper
- Protector
- Introvert
- Extrovert

Your list can be as long as it has to be, just as long as you are being honest with yourself to the best of your ability. Don't worry if your list isn't a long one. Having a short list might actually help you by narrowing things down faster.

Now it's time to take the keywords that you've selected, and think about what they really mean to you. If the word, "leader" was on your list, ask yourself why you feel that you should lead. Do a lot of people look up to you for advice? Do you feel that you can do a better job than many of the leaders out there?

Now try to look for a match between the keywords in this chapter and the answers to the questions from the previous chapter. For example, one of the questions in the last chapter was, " What makes time pass by really fast for me?"

Let's say that helping people, socializing, and meeting new people are all things that help make time go by really fast for you. If being a leader is on your keyword list, you might consider looking into becoming a life coach.

Priority should be given to your best matches.

The Importance Of Trying New Things And Giving Them A Chance

Even when you feel a strong need to pursue something, it doesn't mean that you can't give other things a chance as well. I originally wanted to be a drummer when I was about 11 years old. I could never do my homework for a long period of time without stopping to tap on the desk or textbook with my pencil.

The guitar was just so common. I felt like I would be more original by playing the drums. I thought that I was going to be a drummer, but I decided to give the guitar a chance, regardless of how overly common it is.

It wasn't long before I really got into the guitar, and by the time I was 13 years old, I never looked back. I can be much more expressive with the guitar than I can be with the drums. I have other passions now, but playing the guitar will always be one of them.

When you discover your passion, it won't matter how overly common it might happen to be.

Even when something has already gotten overly popular, everyone still has a chance to put their own perspective on it. You can take something that is commonly practiced, and then take it in a totally different direction.

It can be difficult to know whether or not you are making the right choice before you have even given something a chance.

I wasn't born with any desire to pick up a guitar. I liked certain styles of music when I was 8 years old, but I had no intention of playing an instrument at the time. I simply gave something a chance, and then I found one of my passions.

Don't underestimate what you are capable of.

Something that strikes up a mild interest within you can actually turn into something much bigger later on. But you have to give it a chance first.

There has probably already been at least one time in your life where you didn't know what you were missing out on until you went ahead and tried it.

Even if you don't have a big interest in something at first, you might get the urge to try it out anyway.

Sometimes your passion starts out as just a small urge, so there's no reason to ignore something before you have really tested it out.

The more things you try, the better of an idea you will gain of what your likes and dislikes are. Not everything has to require your undivided attention. To save time, different hobbies can be pursued simultaneously.

Pursuing one hobby full time for a decade while ignoring all of your other interests is simply too big of a risk, unless you are absolutely certain it is what you want to do.

Pay equal attention to all of your dreams and desires, not just the big ones.

Don't neglect a small hobby in favor of a bigger one.

It just might end up leading to something big.

The Number One Thing You Need To Do To Turn Your Desires Into A Career

Even after you have a good idea of what you want to do, you still have to find out how to make a career out of it.

Obviously, becoming a rock star is not for everyone, but now that you have been honest with yourself about your desires, you can more accurately look for something that specifically suits you.

Putting something like "rock star" on your list was just to get you thinking in the right direction. It can allow you to realize that a career in the field of music is calling you. If you try to be too realistic from the beginning, you might find yourself with a blank list.

That's why it's so important to go in order by thinking of your desires first, and then figuring out how you can turn them into reality.

Goals are not accomplished through wishful thinking, but acknowledging the things that you really want can lead you to a career that is right for you.

The number one thing you need to do to turn your desires into a career is to check out your available resources and take full advantage of the ones that appeal to you the most. Almost everything will depend on the amount of accessible resources that you have.

The highest-paying careers are not necessarily the ones that will require the most resources, but the more resources you have available to you, the more likely you will be to achieve success.

Many people have gone to college just for the sake of going to college, and then they end up with careers that have nothing to do with what they went to school for. They went to college because they felt like they had no other resources available to them.

Even though there are no guarantees that you will have a good career after you finish school, many people go to college anyway.

Most of us are told that our resources can only be found at school, so we don't even bother to look elsewhere.

Before you decide to pursue college, trade school, an apprenticeship, or your own business, make sure that you weigh the pros and cons of each one of those things, and then compare your results. Write it all down if you have to.

Having doubts about whether you've made the right choice is normal. Sometimes your fear increases as you get closer to achieving your lifelong dreams.

Positive things don't always feel positive right away, but you have to give them a chance, otherwise you might never know for sure.

Think of it this way:

If you have ever been sick with a cough before, you probably thought of the cough as a bad thing. You might not have realized that a cough is just the body's natural way of handling the flu. A cough doesn't necessarily mean that you are on the wrong path. A cough might be necessary sometimes to help you recover faster by getting rid of germs.

Use your best judgment.

Don't spend years and years going down a path that you strongly feel is not right for you. But don't always be so quick to dismiss something just because you are unsure about it initially.

Those who never find or apply their passion are usually the same ones who always want all of the work done for them.

Those who do find and apply their passion are usually the ones who are willing to go through trial and error.

Take the time to educate yourself, but don't allow yourself to procrastinate. Learn the things that you need to know in order to get started, but don't get caught up in trying to learn everything all at once. Try not to get too far ahead of yourself.

When you plan a vacation, you aren't thinking about the vacation that you will be taking five years from now. You want to focus on the vacation that you are currently taking. All you have to do is plan one trip at a time.

Many people refuse to open their eyes to the resources that are available to them outside of college. Although many job opportunities are eliminated by not finishing college, there are other options.

Some jobs even offer to pay you while you train with them. Instead of paying a school to educate you about your career of choice, you can have a company pay you while they educate you about the job.

There are also jobs that you can obtain a license and/or certification for without having to spend 4 years in college. Some programs can be completed in less than a couple of years.

There was a trade school that I went to where I worked on cars. The duration of the basic program was a year, and then there was an additional course I signed up for to give my resume a boost. The entire thing would have lasted about 15 months, assuming that you don't have to retake any of your courses. I only stayed for a couple of months before deciding that it wasn't for me, but if you have an interest in cars and you can see yourself making a career out of working on them, a school like that might be a good choice for you.

Make sure that you check all of your options. Don't just check all of your options as far as which college you should attend. Check your options inside and outside of college.

If you are certain about what you want to do, and if you know that a certain school will provide you with the resources that you need to succeed, it makes sense to think about going to school. But keep in mind that there are also resources outside of school that might serve you better.

If you are independent and have access to a computer with internet connection, you can already begin to look into something like writing, freelancing, etc. Sometimes a computer might be the best resource available to you.

I'm just trying to get you to think in the right direction. It's all about making the best of what you have to work with. There are other possibilities out there besides school.

I had a friend that was good with computers. Instead of getting a college degree, he decided to open his own electronics business. He didn't have a lot of money to spend on school, but he had a large social network to help him get started on his own business.

In his case, his social network was his biggest resource, and he took advantage of it. Money wasn't his strength, so he made the best out of what he did have.

Being aware of your resources is a good start, but you also have to use them if you want to see results.

It's difficult to be certain whether a resource will be worth your time and/or money until you try it out and give it a chance, but that doesn't have to be a bad thing.

Everyone will have their own opinion about everything, and you can never be sure about something until you have seen and experienced it for yourself.

Life is a journey, and a journey that doesn't allow you to travel at all is a boring one. Sometimes you have to find out what is worst for you before you can truly appreciate what is best for you.

How To Prevent Your Passion From Fading Away

After discovering your passion, you need to make sure that you don't lose it. The worst thing you can do with your passion is to turn it into a huge chore or a job that you hate.

Your passion wasn't meant to just entertain you for a few months, it was meant to add value to the world that lasts a lifetime.

One of the keys to holding on to your passion is to give yourself enough time away from it. Although there are other things that can make your passion fade away, stress always seems to kill it the fastest.

The reason we hate our dead-end jobs so much is not necessarily because they are boring, but because we are overworked.

You can always use your imagination to make a boring job more interesting, but you can't do much of anything when you are feeling stressed out and overworked.

Boredom is a problem that can be fixed through creativity and a positive state of mind, but high-stress situations are very difficult to deal with.

If you want to keep your passion going strong, you have to make sure that you are not being too hard on yourself. The last thing you need when you are trying to nourish your passion is stress.

Another thing that seems to get in the way is a lack of belief in our instincts. We know that we are pursuing the things that are important to us, but we feel like giving up when something goes wrong.

Sometimes we know what we want to accomplish, but we assume that we're not allowed to make mistakes along the way.

When we face tough times, we assume that we must be in the wrong place.

Just because you are not extremely good at the things that you have a passion for right away, it doesn't mean that you are in the wrong place.

Not making a lot of money from your passion right away does not mean that you are in the wrong place.

Getting negative feedback from negative people does not mean that you are in the wrong place. Having a bad day does not mean that you are in the wrong place.

When you are having your doubts about your passion, just remember that your instincts are more important than your skills. Skills can be developed along the way, but you can't change what you were really meant to be.

The idea is to encourage good things to happen without trying to force them to happen.

As I stated earlier, you can turn your passion into a career if you find and take full advantage of your available resources. But you shouldn't be dependent on turning your passion into a huge income stream.

The whole point of being passionate about your work is so that you can enjoy what you are doing while bringing value into the world.

Money shouldn't be your first priority when you are pursuing your passion.

You can pursue your passion without having to give up on everything else in your life. It's not necessary to dedicate 100% of your life to just one single passion. If you try too hard to turn your passion into a career, you will lose interest in it very soon.

Make time for other things in your life and try to balance it all out.

Life is short.

You can't afford to lose sight of the things that are truly important. There are plenty of distractions out there that can easily throw you off course if you allow them to.

There are budgets to balance, finances to be concerned about, and countless other things. We need to find out which things are draining us the most before we can find out how to eliminate the stress that kills our passion.

Whether it's because of stress or anything else, watching the things that you care about the most gradually fall away from you is incredibly discouraging.

If you ever notice yourself losing your drive, take the time to ask yourself these questions:

- Am I taking enough breaks?
- Am I putting too much pressure on myself?
- Am I willing to let go of this stress, and then move on?
- What made me want to find my passion in the first place?
- What made me want to pursue my passion?
- What will most likely happen if I give up?
- How great could the rewards eventually be if I decide to keep on going?

You have to always remember why you're doing this in the first place. Giving up on something that is important to you when things become difficult might take away some of your short-term stress, but it will bring you more stress in the long term.

The next time you feel your passion slipping away, keep these things in mind:

- There are people out there who need you
- There are people who will appreciate you for helping them out through your passion
- The best path isn't always easy at the beginning, but it ends with great rewards
- Taking breaks from your passion can help you restore it
- It takes time to develop the skills for your passion

A lot of people seem to use failure as a reason for not trying at all. They assume that you have to be really good at your passion right from the beginning. Although passion is something that you might have had since the beginning of your life, developing the necessary skills for your passion usually doesn't happen until later on.

Dreams need to have a chance to develop into reality.

Remember, skills and success can be followed by dreams. You don't have to excel at your passion right away. It can be frustrating to not see results when you are putting everything that you have into your passion. There will be good days and bad days.

A bad day is when you, for whatever reason, lose interest in your passion. You lose your motivation and you might feel stressed out, discouraged, or overwhelmed.

The important thing to remember is that these bad days are only temporary. Your passion is not dead. Give yourself a break and regain your inspiration.

Losing your momentum from time to time is not the end of the world. As long as you are on the right path, things will work out in the end.

Understanding The Reason For Your Lifelong Dreams

Some while ago, I believed that you had to be absolutely miserable in order to be successful in life. I was under the impression that you always had to pay a brutal price for something good before you were allowed to experience it.

Although it does take hard work to achieve your lifelong dreams, you shouldn't have to feel miserable the whole time.

Hard work should not be confused with painful work. Hard work is something that you are able to do when you are pursuing your passion. Painful work is dreaded labor that you are forced to do over and over again.

Hard work is when you consistently put a lot of effort into something that you enjoy doing. Hard work involves stress, but it shouldn't stress you out.

The energy just seems to flow naturally, and when you feel like you need a break, you take one. If you feel like you need additional time off, you take it.

Even one day of painful work feels like to much. It doesn't help when you are forced to do dreaded work day after day, year after year. A couple of days off a week and a few week of vacation a year is never enough when you are doing painful work.

The purpose for your lifelong dreams is to make sure that you are taking the right direction in your life.

Even when you're not sure about what you are going to do or how you are going to do something, the desires within you will eventually provide a solution as long as you never stop listening to them. The solution might not come to you right away, and it might not always be exactly what you expected it to be, but when it does arrive, it will be the best thing for you.

Many people think that their lifelong dreams are meant to always remain as fantasies or fairy tales. They don't seem to realize that their lifelong dreams are there for a reason.

Finding your passion and applying your lifelong dreams starts out by listening to your desires, not disregarding them.

You were meant to work, but you were not meant to do painful work. Painful work will make you feel exhausted, agitated, and unproductive.

Even when you are getting a lot of work done, you might still feel unproductive if you hate what you're doing. The work feels painful because you are going in the wrong direction.

Even though pursuing your passion can be scary, it's worth it. Fear can actually seem pretty mild when you compare it to depression.

Fear of failure can be overcome as you accomplish your goals with hard work. But as long as you are dedicating every minute of your time to things that you hate doing, the depression won't go away.

The popular thing to do seems to be forgetting about your dreams altogether, but that doesn't have to be you. There's no need to turn your whole life upside down.

You shouldn't quit your responsibilities or obligations, but you do need to make an effort to keep your dreams alive. Whether it's for an hour a day or 60 hours a week, you need to make some time to pursue your lifelong dreams.

There is nothing wrong with taking one small step at a time. Remember, small things can lead to big things.

Putting too much pressure on yourself can backfire on you anyway. It's more important to not overwhelm yourself.

The resources that you need might not always be available to you right away, but it's important to not let go of your lifelong dreams in the meantime.

Not seeing any results right away does not necessarily mean that your lifelong dreams need to be forgotten; It just means that you need to practice patience, hard work, and persistence.

Have fun on your journey of self-discovery.

More from David A. Hunter

"CREATIVE THINKING: WHEN YOU FEEL LIKE YOU HAVE NO IDEAS."

"HOW TO STOP PROCRASTINATING: START NOW AND DON'T LOOK BACK."

"HOW TO ACHIEVE SUCCESS: TAKE CHARGE OF YOUR DESTINATION IN LIFE."

"HOW TO BUILD CONFIDENCE: BELIEVE IN YOUR TREMENDOUS CAPABILITIES."